ICONS

TUSCANY STYLE

TUSCANY

Landscapes, Terraces & Houses

Interiors Details

STYLE

EDITOR

Angelika Taschen

TASCHEN

KÖLN LONDON LOS ANGELES MADRID PARIS TOKYO

Cover: Venerable walls: Where cooking is a great experience.
Couverture: Murs vénérables : quand la cuisine devient événement.
Umschlag: Ehrwürdige Mauern: Hier wird Kochen zum Erlebnis.
Photo: *Mirjam Bleeker/Taverne Agency*

© 2003 TASCHEN GmbH
Hohenzollernring 53, D-50672 Köln
www.taschen.com

Concept and Layout by Angelika Taschen, Cologne
Cover design by Angelika Taschen, Claudia Frey, Cologne
Project Management by Stephanie Bischoff, Cologne
Texts by Christiane Reiter, Berlin
Lithography by Horst Neuzner, Cologne
English Translation by Klaus Ziegler, Cologne
French Translation by Anne Charrière, Cologne

Printed in Italy
ISBN 3–8228–1642–6

10/11 The vineyard near at hand: The Castello di Gabbiano. *La vigne devant la porte : le Castello di Gabbiano.* Den Weinberg vor der Tür: Das Castello di Gabbiano.
Photo: Eric Laignel & Patricia Parinejad

12/13 A lady made of stone: Wanda Ferragamo's house. *Une dame de pierre : dans la propriété de Wanda Ferragamos.* Eine Dame aus Stein: Auf Wanda Ferragamos Anwesen.
Photo: Reto Guntli

14/15 Cypress Skyline: Garden of the architect P. Castellini. *Horizon de cyprès : dans le jardin de l'architecte P. Castellini.* Skyline aus Zypressen: Im Garten des Architekten P. Castellini.
Photo: Guy Bouchet/Inside

16/17 Diving in happiness: Roberto Budini-Gattai's swimming pool. *Plonger dans le bonheur : la piscine de Roberto Budini-Gattai.* Kopfüber ins Glück: Der Pool von Roberto Budini-Gattai.

18/19 Behind mighty doors: The villa di Tizzano. *Derrière d'imposantes portes : la villa di Tizzano.* Hinter mächtigen Toren: Die Villa di Tizzano.

20/21 It's all symmetry: A garden in Colli Fiorentini. *Tout est symétrie : un jardin dans les Colli fiorentini.* Alles ist Symmetrie: Ein Garten in den Colli fiorentini.

22/23 Kept in style: View of the vineyards. *Un soin exemplaire : les vignes.* Musterhaft gepflegt: In den Weinbergen.
Photo: Gianni Berengo Gardin

24/25 In the sun: Leisa and Michael Snyder's house. *Dans la lumière : la maison de Leisa et de Michael Snyder.* Im Licht: Das Haus von Leisa und Michael Snyder.
Photo: Karsten Damstedt

26/27 Light and shade: In front of Wolfgang Storch's house. *Ombre et soleil : devant la propriété de Wolfgang Storch.* Sonne und Schatten: Vor Wolfgang Storchs Besitz.
Photo: Eric Laignel & Patricia Parinejad

28/29 A beautiful espalier: Gateway up to the hills. *Bel espalier : la porte des collines.* Schönes Spalier: Das Tor zu den Hügeln.
Photo: Eric Laignel & Patricia Parinejad

30/31 Monica Sangberg Moen and Stefano Crivelli's vantage point. *Point de vue chez Monica Sangberg Moen et Stefano Crivelli.* Aussichtsplatz von Monica Sangberg Moen und Stefano Crivelli.
Photo: Eric Laignel & Patricia Parinejad

32/33 A place in the sun: Tuscany invites you to take a seat. *A la lumière du soleil : la Toscane invite à déjeuner.* Im Sonnenschein: Die Toskana bittet zu Tisch.
Photo: Eric Laignel & Patricia Parinejad

34/35 The smell of summer: Herbs and spices, freshly picked. *Les senteurs de l'été : herbes et épices, fraîchement cueillies.* So duftet der Sommer: Kräuter und Gewürze, frisch gepflückt.
Photo: Bärbel Miebach

36/37 Open house: Arturo Carmassi's villa. *Des portes toujours ouvertes : la villa d'Arturo Carmassi.* Wo die Türen immer offen stehen: Arturo Carmassis Villa.
Photo: Mads Morgensen

38/39 Endless avenues: A walk beneath cypresses. *Des allées sans fin : promenade sous les cyprès.* Endlose Alleen: Ein Spaziergang unter Zypressen.
Photo: Mads Morgensen

40/41 In full bloom: Carmassi's garden at dawn. *En pleine floraison : le jardin de Carmassi au crépuscule.* In voller Blüte: Carmassis Garten in der Dämmerung.
Photo: Mads Morgensen

42/43 As though calculated: Way up to Marilena und Lorenzo Bonomo. *Tracé à la perfection : le chemin vers Marilena et Lorenzo Bonomo.* Wie abgezirkelt: Der Weg zu Marilena und Lorenzo Bonomo.

44/45 Green as far as the horizon: The most beautiful views of Tuscany. *Vert jusqu'à l'horizon : les plus beaux aspects de la Toscane.* Grün bis zum Horizont: Die schönsten Seiten der Toskana.

46/47 Geometry: In front of the villa le Carceri. *Notes rondes : devant la villa le Carceri.* Eine runde Sache: Vor der Villa le Carceri.

48/49 In Mediterranean colours: House of the architect P. Castellini. *Dans les couleurs du Sud : la maison de l'architecte P. Castellini.* In südlichen Farben: Das Haus des Architekten P. Castellini.
Photo: Guy Bouchet/Inside

50/51 Resting place under arches: Siesta in Patio. *Repos sous les arcades : la sieste dans le Patio.* Ruheplatz unter Bögen: Siesta im Patio. *Photo: Guy Bouchet/Inside*

52/53 Dinner table for friends: In Maremma. *Table de fête pour les amis : dans la Maremma.* Festtafel für Freunde: In der Maremma.

54/55 A turquoise dream: Pool of the villa La Querciola. *Un rêve couleur turquoise : la piscine de la villa La Querciola.* Ein Traum in Türkis: Der Pool der Villa La Querciola. *Photo: Andreas von Einsiedel*

56/57 Summerhouse with a view: In front of Simone de Looze's house. *Tonnelle et point de vue : devant la maison de Simone de Looze.* Laube mit Aussicht: Vor dem Haus von Simone de Looze. *Photo: Mirjam Bleeker/Taverne Agency*

58/59 Nothing but nature: Relaxation for body and soul. *Tout autour rien que la nature : détente pour le corps et l'âme.* Ringsum nichts als Natur: Entspannung für Körper und Seele. *Photo: Mirjam Bleeker/Taverne Agency*

60/61 Keep things rolling: Playing boules in Tuscany. *Ça roule : jeu de boule en Toscane.* Die Kugel rollt: Boule in der Toskana. *Photo: Mirjam Bleeker/Taverne Agency*

62/63 Perfect swing: Sport Italian style. *Elan parfait : sport à l'italienne.* Perfekter Schwung: Sportstunde auf Italienisch. *Photo: Mirjam Bleeker/Taverne Agency*

64/65 All in red: Poppy in bloom. *Tout en rouge : le coquelicot en fleur.* Ganz in Rot: Der Klatschmohn blüht. *Photo: Mirjam Bleeker/Taverne Agency*

66/67 Green garage: Even the cars take a holiday. *Garage vert : même les voitures sont en vacances.* Grüne Garage: Selbst die Autos machen Urlaub.
Photo: Mirjam Bleeker/Taverne Agency

68/69 Steps to the siesta: At Simone de Looze house. *Marches vers la sieste : dans la maison de Simone de Looze.* Die Stufen zur Siesta: Das Haus von Simone de Looze.
Photo: Mirjam Bleeker/Taverne Agency

70/71 Keeping cool: Shady place under the large awning. *Vaste espace : à l'ombre sous la grande marquise.* Auf voller Länge: Schattenplätze unter der großen Markise.
Photo: Mirjam Bleeker/Taverne Agency

72/73 Tree of life: In front of Brigitte Erm's villa. *Arbre de vie : devant la villa de Brigitte Erm.* Baum des Lebens: Vor der Villa von Brigitte Erm.
Photo: Pep Escoda

74/75 Olive grove of one's own: A house in Maremma. *Avec son oliveraie personnelle : une maison dans la Maremma.* Mit eigenem Olivenhain: Ein Haus in der Maremma.

76/77 Country style cuisine: In front of the villa Montosoli. *Cuisine campagnarde par excellence : devant la villa Montosoli.* Landhausküche pur: Vor der Villa Montosoli.

"…The light fell on marble walls; then on marble floor, interspersed with other stones. Mattresses were put out to air; the house exuded the feeling of summery slumbering abandonment…"

Alfred Kerr in: Du bist so schön! Die Welt im Licht II (1920)

«…La lumière tombait sur les murs de marbre, puis sur le sol de marbre parsemé d'autres pierres. Les matelas avaient été exposés à l'air; tout dans la maison dégageait une impression de somnolence estivale…»

Alfred Kerr dans: Du bist so schön! Die Welt im Licht II (1920)

»…Das Licht fiel auf Marmorwände; dann auf marmornen Boden, mit andrem Gestein durchsetzt. Matratzen lagen zum Lüften gebreitet; alles in dem Haus verströmte das Gefühl sommerlich schlummernder Verlassenheit…«

Alfred Kerr in: Du bist so schön! Die Welt im Licht II (1920)

INTERIORS

Intérieurs   Interieurs

84/85 Leaning back: A glass of wine on the veranda. *Confortablement assis : un verre de vin sur la véranda.* Bequem zurückgelehnt: Ein Glas Wein auf der Veranda.
Photo: Andreas von Einsiedel

86/87 The colour of mauve: Room in Mediterranean style. *La couleur mauve : refuge dans le style du sud.* Die Farbe Lila: Refugium im Stil des Südens.
Photo: Andreas von Einsiedel

88/89 View of the bed: Inside Monica Sangberg Moen and Stefano Crivelli's house. *Coup d'œil sur le lit : dans la maison de Monica Sangberg Moen et Stefano Crivelli.* Blick ins Bett: Im Haus von Monica Sangberg Moen und Stefano Crivelli.
Photo: Eric Laignel & Patricia Parinejad

90/91 Splashes of green: As fresh as nature itself. *Nuances de vert : frais comme la nature.* Akzente in Grün: So frisch wie die Natur selbst.
Photo: Eric Laignel & Patricia Parinejad

92/93 Spacious: Tenuta di Trinoro's kitchen. *Joli cadre : la cuisine de Tenuta di Trinoro.* Schöner Rahmen: Tenuta di Trinoros Küche.

94/95 Handpainted: This bed promises blue dreams. *Peint à la main : un lit à rêver en bleu.* Handbemalt: Ein Bett verspricht blaue Träume.

96/97 Under the sign of the olive: Le Belvedere's kitchen. *Sous le signe de l'olive : la cuisine du Belvedere.* Im Zeichen der Olive: Die Küche von Le Belvedere.

98/99 Abundant with delicacies: Invitation by Leisa und Michael Snyder. *Table riche : Leisa et Michael Snyder invitent.* Reich gedeckt: Leisa und Michael Snyder laden ein.
Photo: Karsten Damstedt

100/101 As if on stage: Inside the villa Ron-cioni. *Comme une scène de théâtre : dans la villa Roncioni.* Wie eine Theaterbühne: In der Villa Roncioni.
Photo: Massimo Listri

102/103 True to original: Mural painting in trompe-l'oeil style. *Fidèle à l'original : peintures murales à la manière des trompe-l'oeil.* Original-getreu: Wandmalereien nach Trompe-l'oeil- Art.
Photo: Massimo Listri

104/105 Frugal and classy: Inside Cesare Rovatti's house. *Sobre et élégant : dans la maison de Cesare Rovatti.* Schlicht und ele-gant: Im Haus von Cesare Rovatti.

106/107 Mixed styles: P. Castellini's living room. *Mélange de styles : le séjour de P. Castellini.* Stilmix: Das Wohnzimmer von P. Castellini.
Photo: Guy Bouchet/Inside

108/109 Dual function: Both wardrobe and treasure chest. *Double usage : à la fois armoire et coffre à trésors.* Doppelt genutzt: Schrank und Schatztruhe zugleich.
Photo: Guy Bouchet/Inside

110/111 Pure relaxation: A night in a four-poster bed. *Détente à l'état pur : une nuit dans un lit à baldaquin.* Entspannung pur: Eine Nacht im Himmelbett.
Photo: Guy Bouchet/Inside

112/113 Under old rafters: Reading room with open hearth. *Sous de vieilles poutres : cham-bre de lecture avec cheminée ouverte.* Unter alten Balken: Lesezimmer mit offenem Kamin.
Photo: Eric Laignel & Patricia Parinejad

114/115 All aglow: Dinner by the fireside. *Tout en rouge : un dîner au coin du feu.* Ganz in Rot: Ein Abendessen am Kamin.
Photo: Eric Laignel & Patricia Parinejad

116/117 Spick and span: Inside the villa Le Carceri. A*stiquée à fond : la villa Le Carceri.* Blitzblank poliert: In der Villa Le Carceri.

118/119 Back to the past: The kitchen of the villa Belsedere. *Regard vers le passé : la cuisine de la villa Belsedere.* Blick in die Vergangenheit: Die Küche der Villa Belsedere.

120/121 Pink table decoration: Nature indoors. *Décor de table rose : la nature pénètre directement dans la maison.* Tischschmuck in Pink: Die Natur kommt direkt ins Haus.

122/123 Behind thick walls: Living like Simone de Looze. *Derrière de gros murs : habiter comme Simone de Looze.* Hinter dicken Mauern: Wohnen wie Simone de Looze. *Photo: Mirjam Bleeker/Taverne Agency*

124/125 Checkered and striped: Effective simple patterns. *Carreaux et rayures : des motifs simples qui font de l'effet.* Karriert und gestreift: Einfach-effektive Muster. *Photo: Mirjam Bleeker/Taverne Agency*

126/127 Well covered: One of Simone de Looze's bedrooms. *Bien couvert : dans une chambre à coucher de Simone de Looze.* Gut zugedeckt: In einem Schlafzimmer von Simone de Looze. *Photo: Mirjam Bleeker/Taverne Agency*

128/129 Sources of light: Sunbeams shining through windows and doors. *Sources de lumière : des rayons de soleil dansent à travers portes et fenêtres.* Lichtquellen: Durch Fenster und Tür tanzen Sonnenstrahlen.
Photo: Mirjam Bleeker/Taverne Agency

130/131 Tidy: A plain wall unit in the room. *Soigneusement rangé : chambre avec éléments de rangement muraux.* Sauber aufgeräumt: Zimmer mit schlichter Schrankwand.
Photo: Mirjam Bleeker/Taverne Agency

132/133 Refreshing: Shower with a view of the garden. *L'élément eau : douche avec vue sur le jardin.* Im nassen Element: Dusche mit Blick in den Garten.
Photo: Mirjam Bleeker/Taverne Agency

134/135 Spacious: Simone de Looze await her guests. *Beaucoup de place : Simone de Looze attend ses invités.* Viel Platz: Simone de Looze wartet auf Gäste.
Photo: Mirjam Bleeker/Taverne Agency

136/137 Venerable walls: Where cooking is a great experience. *Murs vénérables : quand la cuisine devient événement.* Ehrwürdige Mauern: Hier wird Kochen zum Erlebnis.
Photo: Mirjam Bleeker/Taverne Agency

"…The outside wall of my room is coverered with yellow, ripely smelling roses and small yellow flowers, not unlike to dogroses; just growing a bit more quietly and more obediently up the high trellis…"

Rainer Maria Rilke in: Das Florenzer Tagebuch (1898)

«…Le mur extérieur de ma chambre est recouvert de roses jaunes au parfum musqué et de petites fleurs jaunes qui ne sont pas sans rappeler l'églantine sauvage ; elles ne se font qu'un peu plus silencieuses et plus obéissantes en grimpant le long des hauts espaliers…»

Rainer Maria Rilke dans: Das Florenzer Tagebuch (1898)

»…Die Wand meines Zimmers ist nach außen hin mit gelben, reif duftenden Rosen und kleinen gelben Blumen überblüht, die wilden Heckenröschen nicht unähnlich sind; sie steigen nur etwas stiller und gehorsamer die hohen Spaliere hinauf…«

Rainer Maria Rilke in: Das Florenzer Tagebuch (1898)

DETAILS

Détails Details

A MARIA SS. DELLA CI...
PROTEC.GITRICE DE ...
ED A S. VINCENZO FERRE...
QUESTO SACELLO
CON MISTICHE CERIMONIE DE...
IL DI 22 SETTEMBRE DE...
DA MONS. GIUSEPPE T...
VESCOVO DI VOLTERR...
I FRATELLI TANGASS...
...DICARONO

1000

MON MONDE
C'EST moN
DeMoN MoN
MoNdE C'EsT
mOn DeMoN

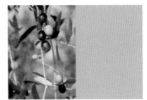

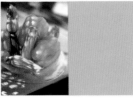

144 Delicacies:
Freshly picked olives.
Un délice: olives
fraîchement cueillies.
Köstlichkeiten: Oliven,
frisch vom Baum.
Photo: Eric Laignel &
Patricia Parinejad

146 Stoneware:
Crockery in Tuscan
colours. *Grès : vais-*
selle aux couleurs de
la Toscane. Steingut:
Geschirr in den Far-
ben der Toskana.
Photo: Eric Laignel &
Patricia Parinejad

147 Two-coloured:
Black and green
olives. *Bicolore :*
olives noires et vertes.
Zweitarbig: Schwarze
und grüne Oliven.
Photo: Eric Laignel &
Patricia Parinejad

148 Rich in vitamins:
Zucchinis and paprika.
Riches en vitamines :
courgettes et poivrons.
Vitaminreich: Zucchini
und Paprika.
Photo:
Karsten Damstedt

150 Ripe: Dark purple
grapes. *Certificat de*
maturité : raisins noirs.
Reifezeugnis: Blaue
Weintrauben.

151 Proud: Statue
of a cock. *Gonflée*
d'orgueil : une statue
de coq. Stolz ge-
schwellt: Eine Hahnen-
statue.

153 Delicacies: Ham,
cheese and bread.
Les délices du palais :
jambon, fromage et
pain. Delikatessen:
Schinken, Käse und
Brot.

154 In rows: Home-
made sauce. *En*
rangées : la sauce
maison. Aufgereiht:
Hausgemachte Sauce.

155 Ripened by the
sun: Tuscan tomatoes.
Mûries au so-leil :
tomates de Toscane.
Sonnengereift: Tos-
kanische Tomaten.

156 Needlework:
Filigree embroidery.
Fait main : broderie de
filigrane. Handarbeit:
Filigrane Stickerei.

158 Memory:
Engraved in stone.
Souvenir : écriture
dans la pierre.
Erinnerung: Schrift
in Stein.
Photo: Eric Laignel &
Patricia Parinejad

159 Framed: Portrait
of a monk. *Encadré :*
portrait d'un moine.
Eingerahmt: Portrait
eines Mönchs.

161 Heraldic ani-
mal: Printed on cloth.
Animal de blason :
imprimé sur tissu.
Wappentier: Auf Stoff
gedruckt.

162 A matter of faith: Antique wall decoration. *Affaire de croyance : décoration murale antique.* Glaubenssache: Antiker Wandschmuck.

163 Picture gallery: Individual souvenirs. *Galerie de tableaux : souvenirs personnels.* Bildergalerie: Persönliche Souvenirs.

165 Play of Colours: Crockery cupboard. *Jeux de couleur : vaisselier à l'ancienne.* Farbenspiel: Neuer alter Geschirrschrank. *Photo: Andreas von Einsiedel*

166 In pairs: Shoes in the entrance hall. *Par deux : collection de chaussures dans l'entrée.* Paarweise: Schuhsammlung im Flur.

169 Silver sheen: Olive twig on linen. *Eclat argenté : branche d'olivier sur lin.* Silberglanz: Olivenzweig auf Leinen. *Photo: Eric Laignel & Patricia Parinejad*

170 Refreshing: Antique stone basin. *Rafraîchissant : bac ancien en pierre.* Erfrischung: Antikes Steinbecken.

171 Noble: sumptuously ornate bathroom. *Point d'eau : une salle de bain richement décorée.* Wasserstelle: Reich verziertes Bad.

173 Turning points: Polished taps. *Invitation à tourner : des ferrures bien polies.* Drehmomente: Polierte Armaturen. *Photo: Mirjam Bleeker/ Taverne Agency*

174 Treasures of the sea: Twisted shells. *Trésors marins : coquillage vrillés.* Meeresschätze: Gedrehte Muscheln. *Photo: Mirjam Bleeker/ Taverne Agency*

175 From the woods: Freshly picked mushrooms. *Messagers de la fo-rêt: champignons fraîchement cueillis.* Waldboten: Frisch gepflückte Pilze. *Photo: Mirjam Bleeker/ Taverne Agency*

177 Accessory: A heavy wine cooler. *Au frais sur la table : un pot qui pèse son poids.* Tischaccessoire: Schwerer Weinkühler. *Photo: Mirjam Bleeker/ Taverne Agency*

178 Fruit bowl: Juicy melons. *As-siette de fruits : melons juteux.* Obstteller: Saftige Melonen. *Photo: Mirjam Bleeker/ Taverne Agency*

179 Just harvested: Chilli and paprika. *Tout juste récoltés : piments et poivrons.* Erntefrisch: Peperoni und Paprika. *Photo: Mirjam Bleeker/ Taverne Agency*

189

181 Spicy: Fresh
garlic. *Assaisonne-*
ment : ail frais.
Gewürz: Frischer
Knoblauch.
Photo:
Mirjam Bleeker/
Taverne Agency

182 Flourishing:
View of the garden.
Floraison : regard sur
le jardin. Aufgeblüht:
Blick in den Garten.
Photo:
Mirjam Bleeker/
Taverne Agency

183 Like pearls:
Coloured boules.
Comme des perles :
boules multicolores.
Perlengleich: Bunte
Boulekugeln.
Photo:
Mirjam Bleeker/
Taverne Agency

184 Withdrawn:
Curtains made of
fine cloth. *Intimité :*
rideaux d'étoffes
délicates. Zurück-
gezogen: Gardinen
aus zartem Stoff.

186 Artworks:
Fabrics embroidered
with loving care.
Œuvres d'art : tissus
brodés avec amour.
Kunstwerke: Liebevoll
bestickte Stoffe.
Photo: Eric Laignel &
Patricia Parinejad

187 Natural:
Flowers in a blue
glass. *Naturel : fleurs*
dans un verre bleu.
Natürlich: Blumen in
blauem Glas.
Photo:
Simon Mc Bride/
Franca Speranza

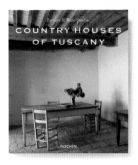

Country Interiors
Ed. Angelika Taschen / Diane
Dorrans Saeks / Hardcover,
304 pp. / € 29.99 / $ 39.99 /
£ 24.99 / ¥ 5.900

Tuscany Interiors
Ed. Angelika Taschen / Paolo
Rinaldi / Hardcover, 288 pp. /
€ 14.99 / $ 19.99 / £ 9.99 /
¥ 2.900

Country Houses of Tuscany
Ed. Angelika Taschen / Barbara
& René Stoeltie / Hardcover,
192 pp. / € 15.99 / $ 24.99 /
£ 12.99 / ¥ 2.900

"Buy them all and add some pleasure to your life."

All-American Ads 40s
Ed. Jim Heimann

All-American Ads 50s
Ed. Jim Heimann

Angels
Gilles Néret

Architecture Now!
Ed. Philip Jodidio

Art Now
Eds. Burkhard Riemschneider,
Uta Grosenick

Atget's Paris
Ed. Hans Christian Adam

Best of Bizarre
Ed. Eric Kroll

Bizarro Postcards
Ed. Jim Heimann

Karl Blossfeldt
Ed. Hans Christian Adam

California, Here I Come
Ed. Jim Heimann

50s Cars
Ed. Jim Heimann

Chairs
Charlotte & Peter Fiell

Classic Rock Covers
Michael Ochs

Description of Egypt
Ed. Gilles Néret

Design of the 20th Century
Charlotte & Peter Fiell

Design for the 21st Century
Charlotte & Peter Fiell

Dessous
Lingerie as Erotic Weapon
Gilles Néret

Devils
Gilles Néret

Digital Beauties
Ed. Julius Wiedemann

Robert Doisneau
Ed. Jean-Claude Gautrand

Eccentric Style
Ed. Angelika Taschen

Encyclopaedia Anatomica
Museo La Specola, Florence

Erotica 17th–18th Century
From Rembrandt to Fragonard
Gilles Néret

Erotica 19th Century
From Courbet to Gauguin
Gilles Néret

Erotica 20th Century, Vol. I
From Rodin to Picasso
Gilles Néret

Erotica 20th Century, Vol. II
From Dali to Crumb
Gilles Néret

Future Perfect
Ed. Jim Heimann

The Garden at Eichstätt
Basilius Besler

HR Giger
HR Giger

Indian Style
Ed. Angelika Taschen

Kitchen Kitsch
Ed. Jim Heimann

Krazy Kids' Food
Eds. Steve Roden,
Dan Goodsell

London Style
Ed. Angelika Taschen

Male Nudes
David Leddick

Man Ray
Ed. Manfred Heiting

Mexicana
Ed. Jim Heimann

Native Americans
Edward S. Curtis
Ed. Hans Christian Adam

New York Style
Ed. Angelika Taschen

**Extra/Ordinary Objects,
Vol. I**
Ed. Colors Magazine

15th Century Paintings
Rose-Marie and Rainer Hagen

16th Century Paintings
Rose-Marie and Rainer Hagen

Paris-Hollywood
Serge Jacques
Ed. Gilles Néret

Penguin
Frans Lanting

Photo Icons, Vol. I
Hans-Michael Koetzle

Photo Icons, Vol. II
Hans-Michael Koetzle

20th Century Photography
Museum Ludwig Cologne

Pin-Ups
Ed. Burkhard Riemschneider

Giovanni Battista Piranesi
Luigi Ficacci

Provence Style
Ed. Angelika Taschen

Pussy Cats
Gilles Néret

Redouté's Roses
Pierre-Joseph Redouté

Robots and Spaceships
Ed. Teruhisa Kitahara

Seaside Style
Ed. Angelika Taschen

Seba: Natural Curiosities
I. Müsch, R. Willmann, J. Rust

See the World
Ed. Jim Heimann

Eric Stanton
Reunion in Ropes & Other
Stories
Ed. Burkhard Riemschneider

Eric Stanton
She Dominates All & Other
Stories
Ed. Burkhard Riemschneider

Tattoos
Ed. Henk Schiffmacher

Tuscany Style
Ed. Angelika Taschen

Edward Weston
Ed. Manfred Heiting

ICONS